Heroes

To
Neil and Penny,

Keeping the candle burning, as you once put it, Neil.

Chris

Heroes

Chris Hurford

Polygon
EDINBURGH

© Chris Hurford 1993

First published by Polygon
22 George Square
Edinburgh

Set in Linotron Sabon
by Koinonia, Bury and
printed and bound in
Great Britain by
Redwood Press Ltd.,
Melksham, Wiltshire.

British Library Cataloguing in
 Publication Data
Hurford, Chris
 Heroes
 I. Title
 821'. 914

ISBN 0 7486 6143 3

The Publisher acknowledges
subsidy from the Scottish Arts
Council towards the publication
of this volume.

Contents

I Heroes

John Wayne	3
The Frame of Things	5
The Hero	6
The Strawberry Man	8
Leontes	9
Canute	11
Macbeth	12
Aeneas	13
The Stronger	14
Caravaggio	15
Bureau Canzone	16
The Frog Prince	19
Ray	20
The Fathers	21

II Men and Women

The Weatherman	27
Again	28
The Querist	30
Now Metaphor	32
Warehouses	33
A Near Miss	34
True Oneness	35
Lies	36
Gravity	38
You Came	40

The Long Thread	41
Young Love	42
Love Poem in English	43
Greek	44

III The Myth of Freedom

An English Rose	47
What We Won the War For	48
The Dumbless Beast	50
Love Poem, Spring	51
Looking at Parkland	52
The Network	54
The Fairground is Allowed	56
Note From the Underground	60
Oranges	61
West	62
Desert Crossing	64
The Border	65
Easter, Warsaw	66
Sin	67
Dreaming of Freedom	68
The Forest	69
Sparrowhawk at Dusk	70
The Book on Coral	71
At the End of Our Lives	72

Acknowledgements

Many of these poems have been previously published in: *The Times Literary Supplement, Verse, The Rialto, The Literary Review, Orbis, The North, Contra-Flow, Helikon (Poland) and Bis (Poland).*

Some of these poems are included in the shared volume LOVE/HATE (Ex-Libris Press, Lublin, Poland, 1991) with Tomek Kitlinski. Artwork by Darek Fodczuk.

Thanks to the Harper-Wood Scholarship Committee, St John's College, Cambridge.

For my father, and for his.

I. Heroes

JOHN WAYNE

(for Simon John)

John Wayne and I strode through the doors,
were crusty-dusty with everyone in the bar
(except the Flesh-Valley Girls),
and pulled on double bourbons
as grittily as gunshot wounds.

Much later we panned out into the street.
John soothed his horse, stroked it like an expert,
but I couldn't be bothered,
and just swung across mine.

Frantic riding! Me and the horse were terrified.
Bumping and sweating, we blindly went
where neither of us had been before.
John rode like the arms of railroad engine wheels,
sliding for miles.
I was too busy hanging on
to look at the hills.

He shot the Indians as they
stood up to fire,
so that when we ripped
into the tepees
there was no one there
except the women.

John scanned them, and switched back out.
He's got a girl in Kalamazoo.
I was momentarily abashed
when one slipped her top and stood up naked,
but quickly chucked her chin
and straddled out too,

then slapped a flank
and rode away with Wayne
towards Sun-Down in the desert.
On and on in a cloud of dust,
and I didn't turn to look back once.

THE FRAME OF THINGS

I remember Mr Coley, the caretaker,
banging yet more nails into the frame
at the bottom of our hopelessly sloping
football field. Playing on a mountain,
he said, improved our aim.

But not mine. I was in goal a lot,
stuck on the line, fearing the collapse
of those listing posts that made
ferocious strikers fluff square shots.

The space they held was precious,
and not only for my eager team,
for I could see my opposite number
eyeing my school and friends and father
as they all huddled into the frame.

And when it finally slid sideways
to nothing we were mid-match.
As the ball rolled like a head down the pitch
I rushed out madly with my back behind me

and kicked the whole wobbling thing, hitched it
clean up, as smooth as a satellite.
Looped over forty two stunned eyes
it hung there, far above the hedge.

THE HERO

A sort of symmetry in the dull thuds
that held his life in their own.
Although they were still deadly, he had grown
to be disappointed, remembering the field next door,
and, with no one home,
a pocketful of 'duds', matches, two stolen fags
and someone else: his first ever.
They had risked explosions, had sent
two huge clods, implausibly graceful,
rearing through the air above the garden.
They turned slowly, hung there, and fell back
into the present.

The trenches that he now digs refill,
each turn blunting him in an exotic clay.
Soft bodies slip back after one strange gesture
into the soft heap; a landscape of lovers,
quietly sleeping after an ecstasy of fumbling.
Their white limbs are gently rolled
by the weight of others falling,
are studded by the useless hooves.

He was being made a god,
an orchid in the delicate loam,

feeding on the soils and sub-soils of abandonment
until his honourable death
for his eager female,
and for all of us who demand
that gross and indelicate act.
Entwine the recently deported hero
with misery and sorrow!
Flung into the arms of everyone and anyone,
he justifies once more the mass of us,
and our fragile pairs.

THE STRAWBERRY MAN

Crecy was ok but he preferred Vietnam
and he didn't want to come back
but he had to so he came to England
and nurtured rotten strawberries and once black
and sick and growing death he'd
get down on all fours or on his back
and try to nibble them to their necks.

The ones he called mommy
his beauties or private jack
simmons were those which bled all-health
in the sun but when you rolled them back
a turned eye, soft hairs
and the real grey brain grinned back.
He sniggered like the rot and remembered finding
Private Jack Simmons.

LEONTES

'You've grown a beard!'
'Many turns of the mind, I guess.'

Love is so thick that if you stop
stirring it settles immediately
and keeps the spoon upright, stranded,
and to itself.

'I'm having such a good time. And last night
I got so drunk that Paul almost had to carry me
home.'

Imagination had tried to create her,
and was destroyed by telephone calls.
And in those very seconds, as I was travelling my wallpaper –
some close pub and faces talking to her
and all the while her shoulders, elbows,
lap and damp subconscious toes
moved in darkness or a fabric half-light
as she talked to the faces now leaning
to the attraction of her clothes.

I am not jealous of her,
but of the places that have her.

'Your eyes look darker. Don't they, Paul.
Don't you think it makes his eyes look darker?'

I've been wandering. Climbing the gates of fields,
making wood pigeons moan at night,
lifting the lids of toads at morning.

'Could we go somewhere on our own?' she said.

How can she, after all this?

Innocence makes me gawkish.

CANUTE

He sat watching TV, his body
blown into the position it was in.
His violence was more violent,
as an ignored son,
with his tongue locked,
when the waves began to touch him.

His thin jaw expected his parents to come.
His people buttoned their coats
and began to go, to leave him
watching TV on a seat on a beach
where the sarcastic wind
brought waves to his feet.

The sky before him sickened
and, flinging gulls away,
pulled over clouds of blood and bruises.
Waves like crumpled sheets
stretched back their throats
and were driven on to meet him.

The TV flickered in his eyes.
This was no end for a king,
to sit squeezing out
a life of shaving foam
hard against his palm.

We left when the waves
had sorrowfully kissed his knees,
when the sky was flooding his face
with tears of pity to match
his tears of rage.

MACBETH

The boy's buried eye
watched the trees and pillars,
the night-time punishers,
jostle for a place to loom.

The ceiling swells down
to fill his mouth.

A light –
the boot that holds the door open
pouts like a cod.

Mother leaves the house,
and hurries away at dead-night.

AENEAS

In Saudi, with your father's toenail
flicked half-off by a cattlegrid
or gatepost, you did not flinch
but calmly dealt with it, while others
quailed and left him to bellow alone.

And now I lie, also in pain,
listening to Pattimore's white bull
in the dark field, hoof-deep in mist,
offering its cold-cudded moan to the moon.
Now I am that ridiculous myth

which you have always had to bear;
the sleepless, obsessed Aeneas
whom you must quieten for fear
of a sudden loss, a departure,
but whom you'd much rather ignore just now

for sleep. Drifting off, you gently elide
my captivating metaphors,
and become that rich unbearable fact
before which I become a fiction.
I will have left you by morning.

THE STRONGER

You, you with no feeling
with heavy shoulders
and a forthright gaze
and a liking for work
and stone and people.

And I a trembling leaf,
who could no more bear
the sickening smack of the world
than a sleeping face.
I am worse – a ball of paper,

a tender useless mouth,
who would now willingly kneel
to comfort and keep you,
or to eat if I could
your red raw mortar brick.

CARAVAGGIO

Others, more aware of human life,
depict epiphany in dark corners
of churches. Briefly lit by a coin,
a knife becomes apparent for a moment –
a dull gleam, some false idea,
too grand a hope, a smile.

BUREAU CANZONE

My man, sing me a simple song.
Sing to me strongly a sweet canzone
of simple statements, solid letters,
at the bureau, before I go on up.

O Bertrans jongleur,
singing of perfections,
of his seven Beauties,
screaming 'twixt his teeth
'We accept your trial offer, and therefore gladly'
The vase was cracked ON ARRIVAL
'Sir, I must strongly...'
Strongly, jongleur, strongly –

| 25 JUN | Southfields | AC | 20.00 | | 749.49 |
| 26 JUN | 100018 | CC | | 650.00 | 1399.49 |

| 26 JUN | Balance to Sheet no 35 | | | | 1399.49 |

and so, at last,
'Are you coming up?', and so,
but secretly Bertrans sings
'beautiful...it hurts...I cannot say...
I write you, I love you'
swearing 'twixt his teeth
'scibo te, just as you are.'
just as she is
just as exactly
just as my ass

The back of the head, tilted slightly,
thinning, domed, unseen, combed,
moved around the blank corner.
The corridor was now empty.
Was he really there once, walking?
Did he tread the end after passing
the place where now empty he had seen
the distant corner, an end,
which he now turned, and was gone?
Did the vital place pass so quickly,
when he was who he was, with eyes
fixed so fatally on the end?

'Off for days, apparently, tracking animals in the
snow, and was fond of reading.
Is that so, Mrs – ?'
'What has happened – disappeared?'
But she didn't tell them of the time when ...

The things people believe in.

In gentle dusk oak leaves smooth
the pink setting sky with stars.
Parents downstairs settle, but past
the open window, fields sweat sweetly
a little, as on tiptoe at the glass we see we see
not Benson's stable, tired nag, old hills,
but a lake, never there, like a plate of milk,
and one long boat with someone standing,
turning

'He did say'

that turning quickly round
he could see the fading shape of Jesus,
and other fancifuls.

All looks since empty: stable, nag,

'We should find him, madam'
crouching
on the first stair
as Bertrans jongleur
on his seventh Provençal Beauty,
scribbling words to burst to music,
with bitten lips, for his one lady, Maent,
who moved away.
She moved – not her.
KEEP STILL OR KEEP AWAY
Strongly, jongleur, strongly

and, at last, the last
letter to the plumber.
And so to bed – go on up,
leaving your canzone to be posted
while I shift downstairs strongly
in the lost, lost dark.
No man, for no woman,

guilty of nothing more than

THE FROG PRINCE

A magnificent Cambridge college court
hides toads in stones; a frog-eyed bright spark
is grovelling with his trousers down, caught short
retching in the men's room, in the dark.

A flagging blue-blooded tongue lolls over
a historic, crested toilet rim,
and the cold eighteenth-century walls are covered
with whatever fizz has just left him.

After the big sweat he is now dry-skinned,
and moans into the damp ceramic
like a blinking, white, reptilian thing
praying down a whelk's hearing trumpet.

But he can't appeal to the ocean.
His unnatural cries find their course
to the sewers the privileged shit in.
Is he drinking, or seeking his source?

Privileged? But he's only a doctor's son –
ordinary school, not very handsome, plays rugger,
well-mannered, smart in brogues, and, like everyone,
attends the annual Decency Dinner

where men, being boys, toad-like grope girls
and vomit decently together.
This one is kissed and blessed as the cool flush swirls,
then rises refreshed from his creature.

RAY

(*for Florence Ellen Betts*)

Shadowy, he stood at the bottom of the bed,
in a cloud of blue tobacco smoke,
obscured by brilliance and bars of sunlight.
His hair slicked back, and ready for a walk.

And he had that look on him,
that surprised, affronted grin,
tilting like a beaten tree
across his long ploughed field of a face.

Apparently I'd promised, last night
I'd promised, and here I was, still dreaming,
missing the early worm, the postman,
an awesome breakfast with him.

But all this was lost on me
as he moved forward into the daylight,
so I turned to dither in another dream
of a lost chiaroscuro by some Old Master.

An alchemist in his study at dawn,
offers a retort and a crucible
to his snoring apprentice. The boy dreams
of dust or nothing after a night's failed vigil,

but the old man motions
to the blackened alembic, saying:
Here's the pestle and here's the sunlight.
It's all you need, now make gold – make it!

THE FATHERS

I. The soil – yes, he tasted it,
the speechless now much sought-for yokel.
He'd chew on a nugget of word-turd
and spit it out - an instant Anglo-Saxon jewel.
It proclaimed wisdom, but it meant sod all.

Next the dusty seed, stored in a dark place
for centuries. Husks of spiders guarded sacks.
Fear and ignorance, a family Bible. He took
his trusty shovel and dug, stooping and farting
like a pump. He'd plant by rule of thumb and finger,

then a swift caress of the damp topsoil
as if to rub it better. Grandmother never minded
all his goings-on, his sowing and his reaping.
Something for nothing from the well-used loam.

The blind seed squirmed, tended by indifference
or silence or just one craved-for word
that shook it thankful to its earth.
Roots fumbled. Home.

II. Two shots in the dark, 10 ml of jissom,
and another branch of the family blossoms.
Now this latest Spring bloom burgeons –
unhumbled and bored, his mind honed and refined
to the point of a pillow. While he wallows he ponders
as to whom he should offer his cold turned shoulder.

Or reading under canopies and bowers
he listens with the rest to Handel's Messiah,
and having no specific function ever,
is asked to appreciate the asphodels
severed but gorgeous, plunged into deep water.
Their corpuscles stiffened and stuffed with sugar.

He wonders, this dazzling gem,
this needlessly brightened Chaunticleer,
if a word is worth anything to a deed,
and how he himself came to be so worthless,
when he hears an urgent whisper hiss:
Jim, could you light the chandelier?

III. Meanwhile his oldest surviving relation
loses all sight and hearing,
curls up into a ball (embarrassing),
and dies. Skin has shrivelled
around the teeth and bone,
the penis to its corm,

and the final breath to a stifled yawn
that takes him by surprise. Was this
his first aspiration to a flood of passion?
Four days later this mouth is filled
with rich dark soil that his own wife shovels
in at the graveside without compassion.

And what to make of such a collapse,
this crumbling of nothing, or very seeming
little? For those who loved him,
whose own strong selves were echoed and tested
in the cavernous well, their love
was deepened and was enough.

For others, who needed a love to grow
before they could grow into themselves,
who called out their names and heard no answer,
there is an open grave that words can't fill.
Deeds are worn to the finger,
thoughts wearied to the bone.

Roots dangle in the meaningless,
and the very earth is treacherous.
A blackbird batters something on a stone,
and a robin on the obligatory spade
wrings silver requiems from the air.
The snail escapes to follow its own mucus trail,
blindly seeking home.

II. Men and Women

THE WEATHERMAN

The weatherman said it would be a clear night
and a fine tomorrow, although clouds boiled over
the London studio.

The waiter of our table for two
poured the wine with gusto
from a great height,

just as you were saying that
loneliness is being free without rejoicing.
I half-suggested coffee. You couldn't wait.

My fine filigree did not disappear,
as I'd hoped it would,
when we took my clothes off.

Gazing up from the floor, I saw that
the stars and the night were clear,
as he has said,

though dew was falling to earth
like rain. It touched the window,
the gutter, the streetlight's halo.

And while you hid yourself to cry
I openly wept,
which you thought was good.

You spilt my wine when you moved me,
and it seeped across the carpet.
In the morning, in our sad embrace,

we listened to the blackbird singing,
with dew on its back, to the milkman
entering the drenched gardens.

AGAIN

I. A door had punched her in the eye!
And although again it was still sudden.
Breathtaking. She could hardly stand
or believe it. Then a slam and a silence

and a solitude for no reason.
Then the hoped-for by him dull
visceral ache, and the guilt,
and hate and spells of tinnitus

which ceased to be a problem
when the phone began to ring
incessantly. If she answered
there was a click and a purr.

After seven weeks she craved for speech.
After eight, the recorded sound of a baby
crying. Memory and pity were all
this plaintive plea, while he aroused her

to tears, to storm. He loathed
her seeming high calm wire act
that dared against love's weakness.
Exhausted of course she called, unclear.

He said 'Now we're talking'.
That tender voice at her ear.

II. After everything – scenes in restaurants,
tortured napkins, even tears from him –
now appeased, reconciled, peaced.
Tenderness and old days.

She went singing to the bathroom pleased
and poured the bath milk
from its silky globe of skin.
He sat like a boy on the sofa, waiting.

Two months has made the room a shrine
and she precious almost holy.
He cast about to make her lounge his own.
Tried not to feel jealous of her bathroom.

The steaming water was no more strong solace
but her longed-for rightful ceremony.
Its tact, its obeisance, its gentle
privileged ministry.

Later she would rise, robed in milk
and towels and he thought mystery
to likewise slip between the teeth
of servitude and mastery.

THE QUERIST

Winter rain spattered the window
of your high-up one-room flat.

We basked on the bed
like lizards, cooling our tongues,

admiring our skins; or lounged
before the fire half-dressed,

domestic and debauched.
That low erotic lamp was apt

to highlight your falling hair
as you bent to mend a tear

in your recently abandoned skirt.
But by now my interest

in your neck and breasts was missing
the point completely. You expertly

speared a needle with a gathered thread,
and later you casually offered

to remove at last that stubborn thorn,
buried deep in my palm

for over a year. The storm
shook the whole house slightly.

The needle was a patient,
trembling querist,

a delicate pilgrim, a burning question.
It moved into my skin, past nerve

and bone. Its tiny bloodied point
felt deeper, searching for an answer.

My dull pulse thudded its monotone:
'There's none. There's none.'

NOW METAPHOR

Kinder to my ordinary wicker chair than me you sat.
It crackled like a dried-up desert plant,

and my great love for you, with pangs, burst into flames.
The blaze could hardly be contained.

But now that is over, and this is only metaphor.
These colder nights the complex wood contracts,

tensing into a tighter knot,
noting every drop in temperature.

WAREHOUSES

In from the sea rolls a ship's horn,
forlorning the docky arenas.
Blast-ended cables and orange neon gone
prickly on the puddled concrete.

There is a wet wind of recent rain
blowing over from the hills at our backs,
blowing wide and empty through the inky spaces,
and on through the empty streets.

And here we are, in damp coats, with cold hands,
in a car, sat apart,
plucking off leaves to hurriedly patch over
our dangerous warmths.

So we keep the vital distance,
like warehouses.

A NEAR MISS

It was going to be
a difficult departure,
one way and another,

and things had been getting a little
equivocal
over the restaurant table.

The slowly melting candles
and the Irish rock oysters
on their in-shore bed

of dark seaweed
had left me with an urgent need
to quibble,

so I harangued the waiter
and the maitre d'
as to the distance a wild,

homecoming salmon must travel.
Unimpressed, you paid the bill
and smiled,

knowing that a miss
in the long run
is as good as a mile.

TRUE ONENESS

She defined
a union of hearts
as the making of babies
in a field, in a storm,
just outside Waverham, Herts.

'We are one.' She went crazy,
my hand over her mouth.
'More, more, I feel babies.'
I felt the cold front
coming in from the north.

'True oneness, you know,
that's what it is.'
Afterwards I fed her the sandwiches,
which she grabbed and ate heartily,
feeding up for the pregnancy.

Blue numbness
I found
in South Waverham, Herts.

It was a mystical pregnancy;
she became Mother
and I became dad,
or even a little sad, she thought,
for I could never know
that magic feeling of 'other'.
'Never mind,' I said, 'I guess it's too bad,'
mentally noting for next time
the use of a rubber.

LIES

(*for Marina Tsvetayeva*)

The only discernable truths in the world
are the songs of a woman
and the lies of a man.
The former laments the latter
and proves its strength,
its power to endure,
greater than any man.
But why all this heroism?
Love is not some ineffable truth,
and nor is truth.

I am tired, for example, of being humbled
by your humility.
It is as if 'I love you'
is the seal of truth,
and not to love as you do is a crime.
These are the lies of the martyr:
'I cannot live without you'
'Yes, it's nice weather'
'I shall not stop loving you'
'I shall put up with fire'.
Such falsehoods make up truth –
sainthood, family, undeniable life.

It is no wonder then that I,
refusing to tell the lie,
feel embattled, scarred and scared
because if there is no lie,
then all love is delusion.

I love you as I love you,
and only as I can truly admit –
I love you in confusion;
carefully measuring the distances
that proclaim what true love is.

The only discernable truths in the world
are the lies of a woman
and the songs of a man.
The latter laments the former,
and proves its eternal strengths
and failures.
Thus all this heroism and myth.
Love is not some ineffable truth,
and nor is truth.

GRAVITY

Ce monde rayonnant de metal et de pierre (Baudelaire)

Yes, I had been here before.
I knew the geography.
I pushed back the door
of my now lethal room,

thinking of Caesar in his dusty sandals,
of Pizarro, single-minded in the saddle,
and of how I thought I knew
a Rubicon when I saw one.

My head swam. She was a treasure, a gem,
a pearl on a draylon cushion.
I circumnavigated the usual rocks and lures,
the warmed and scented gold and silver,

the turquoise, azure,
and her unfathomable amber.
But she knew I was only testing the water,
not wishing to go under,

for resting an elbow on her raised knee,
her dropping wrist
became an idle question mark
that lightly toyed with my only bauble –

a tinny, insipid schoolboy globe.
Yellow marked the land. Blue marked the sea.
I could never have brought myself
to throw it away.

When she laughed and released it
with the tip of her finger,
the sphere went spinning far beyond me.
There was a silence

as I watched it
sail into infinity,
then another as I succumbed
to her centre of gravity.

YOU CAME

You came at my room's empty hour.
The lamp-stand struggled.
The chair, I know, tried to rise
and answer you.

THE LONG THREAD

Sunlight fades,
and my footsteps in the forest
begin to fill with dew.
The branches that I brushed past
are touched by the moon.
These are the traces of my passing.

Already I am forgotten by the fox
that watched me from the brake.
The hillside where it now leaps
is already forgotten by me.

A sun begins to wake you,
but here night seals me in.
I will be all but smothered
by the dark.

My thoughts reach out too far.
Where are you?
But when we parted I gave you a thread,
so that I would not get lost.

YOUNG LOVE

After my journey where obese ladies
blew their noses in my face,
where lobsters worked on the road outside
under this summer, this tight-clampt furnace
of the horror of summer,
of the longing to be elsewhere,
of the boredom of getting there,
I now walk cooly in the fields
beneath your village.

The railway darkens, the M1 aches away,
and I often look up to the few houses
on the rise, hiding the sea,
and the steep stars just behind.

LOVE POEM IN ENGLISH

(for A.H.)

The rain whispers in the garden's mouth
and chants, wordless but not soundless,
a song of sadness, leaving, drought.
Of words that wandered weightless.
Of a precious breath that lost its people.
Of bloated tongues that lolled, unable
to bear the taste of poetry.

So rain I hear you, and sing early
to the woman who lies near me
the few words that I have left me –
not Faxart, Plastic or Beauty,
not Heaven, Love or Democracy,
but her name, mine, and one covered by a cloth,
its meaning mercifully unclear to both of us.

GREEK

God's old bones
lay on the sand
beneath the wheeling hawk
and the crumbling cliff.

At the water's crinkling edge
we played Adam and Eve.
Tired old me, I thought you didn't mean it,
I thought I should return to the towels.

But you did and you came smiling
out of the sea,
stepping through the air
like the first woman in the world.

III. The Myth of Freedom

AN ENGLISH ROSE

The cat comes only at night,
when everyone else is sleeping,
whilst I am eating, or reading quietly.
She assiduously cleans herself,
laps her fur, smoothes her whiskers,
and then regards me slowly.
She is old; her drowsing eyes blink,
and almost close.

There's life in her yet, though –
she has worms.
If you lift her tail
you can see them; creamy, moving,
sometimes three, more usually two,
spreading like blooms from a bud.

Outside a distant siren wails.
She waits for it to fade, and close,
then blinks again unmoved.
There's nothing more silent
than a flowering rose.

WHAT WE WON THE WAR FOR

'It was presumably a part
of what you grandads were all fighting for –
a restful supper at The Rupert Brooke,
and then a stroll back to my student quarters
amidst church bells and Sunday papers.
The summer, my girlfriend (future wife) –
I felt rich, as if I'd inherited all this.
Even Bach seemed somehow British.

And then – a Spitfire! Tiny, circling,
almost disappearing to become sublime,
doing the Trinity Great Court run,
but far up on a spiral staircase,
saluting those heroes, those aspiring souls
with a halo or a wreath
(a victory role either way).
The veteran growl of pistons and oil,
a cause to fight for and a woman at home:
to those tourists, Englishmen and me underneath,
too young to put one foot on the stair,
it told us what we should be grateful for.'

But there were other signs of the old guard remaining,
as you walked under the thick cloud cover
which that night smothered most of Britain.
An upper-middle class man's son,
straight from the suburbs' democracies,
drunk and staggering with his trousers down.
A real Lord Haw Haw,
but with no stables or estate,
whipping the walls with his leather belt:
'Yield, bitch, yield.' Shirt-tails and legs
were white lillies in the dark
for his father's business,
for the love he missed,
crying as he whipped the ground:
'False start, damn you, false start.'

THE DUMBLESS BEAST

An old hulky coat with a lunatic's shaved head.
His yabber mouth has picked up butts
but c-c-can't get them out.
Groob groob.

At a window he smothers his ghost
which the TV burns through,
and chews on the after-dinner left-overs
of those who spoke all they had to say
with their mouths full.
He mums Darling Dachshund Dear Old Dickie
THERE'S A MAN AT THE WINDOW!
then shambles off for pardon
at the bottom of the garden.
Sitting by a still-smoking pile of leaves
with the last twittering bird
he gets wrapped up in The Times.

He's in your garden, Barbara.
He's just rolled against your shed, George.
But they have already yawned and dragged
their tired tongues and lives to bed.

Later he will crawl quietly
up through the house
to lie at their feet –
an animal footstool
for the heraldic dead.
A dumbless beast,
to hear dreams and feed fears.
He lies watchful. His mere breathing
whispers absolution in their ears.

LOVE POEM, SPRING

There is no empyrean 0, no human mouth
for the burgeoning heart. Devoid of tongues,
you have long since withered into decency, stunned
by your desire to be held, gently captive. Victims
self-willed, touching numbly the ragged cut
at the accustomed root.

In time the inane will taste better to us all.
Buds strain against the frost. Enforced, we insist
on our deformities, and the ice persists.
The stem receives the shrivelled buds again.
My love for you, and particularly for one of you,
sticks in my craw.

LOOKING AT PARKLAND

Out here in thick pasture, pleasant parkland,
that scums the poet's church. Sitting like a native on nails,
musing in fat clover, and suddenly there's a violence
in the air, sweeping up the deeds and thoughts
and words of us who sit luxurious,
blind to the unseen pains that run like contours
above green fields. And I'm swept up
with these flexing waves which form
in the grey space of England,
and am spun round
with the swallows, big-wheeled over the oaks and elms.
But I get sick and giddy with this rising, falling,
and try to clutch thick pasture
which squeals like frightened wealth.
I'm carried like a rag doll up high again
to squiggle signs helplessly on the air's grey pane.
They drip steadily back to earth.
Red on green, and then just green.

I wake at sunset
and only the insects and stems
nod their tiny heads
in tiny circles like echoes,
or the last of the rain.

Then I jump up, remembering –
but ever watchful, you caring gaolers
quickly breathe your kiss of ether,
whispering: 'Its over, it was nothing.
This is England, little worrier.'
I can look but, reclining to my ease, things fade,
and I'm slowly made powerless to remain ungrateful.

Dear,
Did you know that I am practising the ancient art of
    poetry,
but will probably be found drowned in the river, the deep
brown river, after I abandoned my people, and they me,
    and my young heart has been irreparably br   kn

So, in this quiet vale in my twilight sleep,
trying to quieten the pains of birth,
I almost hear the blackbird's perfect music,
but hear:

attic tic tic o shape that fair itude be rede rede men
and marl over rr marble and maidens over and over
with bra and the branches beauty trodden thou silent
form dost tease us out and out of thought as doth tern
tern eternity: cold pastoral!

THE NETWORK

The night freight train,
a nervous bitten flank,
shudders free of the network.
The Deputy Station Manager
sees off this last behemoth,

glowers, coughs, spits and locks
the technological box
that changes points and switches,
and thereby grants our complex wishes.

The right to choose, that's the important thing
to him, the Deputy Station Manager,
and this servant of freedom at 2.10 am
spurns the self-determined night freight train
which picks up speed past the suburb's sleepers.

The dim-lit sidings limply concede
like deserted possibilities.
Yawns to bed, the Deputy Manager's head,
but he kicks and tosses in his dreams, pleads:

Take this fretty network from my brow!
I'm too unfree and too old now.
The curse of keys and interstices!
I want a comet's blazing trail
to hound down the splitting seam of dawn,

a furrowed thought, a fierce intent,
to score the narrow tangent
between night and Hell's embankment.
Oh, the fire in the throat and thought
that longs to love and rage!

He wakes up sweaty after this
to the gentle pop and hiss
of his wife's belaboured epiglottis,
and the simple binary kaaa and fff
of her as yet unwasted breath.

So in the cold and bluey dawn
he stumbles human out of bed,
frail and naked in his familiar room,
to dress and eat and face again
the day's democracies,

with its integrated functions
that weave the web of all our freedoms,
the network's intercommunications,
for us bound and sticky citizens.

THE FAIRGROUND IS ALLOWED

I. The city is white. Snow.
A brief scratch,
and the pen is lifted off the page.
The fairground is allowed.
For one night only.
On wasteground.

And we swarm to it – the warm spot.
The diesel and the wicked machines
have opened up a permitted wound
for the red and hellish in us.
And even though we're lovers,
and can each night cling together,
we descend to embrace this brave crowd,
this heated crowd, flying in the face
of their own obvious evening
on waltzers, ghost trains, merry-go-rounds.

II. Past the steaming stalls and hot dog stands
the gypsy in her caravan,
with her mystery charts and tarot cards,
is hunched over some muddy teacup.
'The truth' (we itch and edge)
'appears in many guises,
but finally resolves itself as – '
dregs, as lies, as tealeaves.
Such is the wisdom that makes us blind
and her dark; pretending all her days
to struggle to see what lies
in the black and abyss-ward ways

of what is now and is to come.
She belies but now believes
that there's something
in seeing nothing.

III. To pounding music mad dodgem cars
like hogs run free to run one way –
that is round. And the crashes are petites-morts!
Yes! The ones we survive and live to crash again.
Metal hits metal as if we can touch
the crush of all things collapsing;
the thrill of the Coke can flattened in the hand,
or the moment the suicide knows he's truly alive,
and slams against the pavement.

In another tent, the slavery of ice-skaters,
dreaming of their diurnal course,
the communal path, on slender blades.
Swans revolving on a delicate lake, then
slam, and the truly alive yob
breaks all icy spells and gets,
if not blood, then tears off little girls
to see if they're divine,
or something that hurts.

IV. And now we fly,
huddled in love on our Ferris seat,
rising out of the churned earth
until there is just you and I,
gulping at our lightness,
me bravely shaking my fist:

Upwards! Yes! Rise on the heat
of the fiery pit!
The stars seem nearer, graspable;
the dark snow whiter, the city laughable.
We exult in our individual crime
and stream towards the highest point
where we shall leave, detach, become sublime.

But we seem to slow, and stop.
We are denied our victory at the steep top.
Now there is only a slight breeze,
perfect calm. The air is thin and pure.
We gaze our separate ways, and sadness
divides us like two moons.
In the absence of our reckless breaths
silence uncares – neither allows nor forbids,
but simply neglects us.
The machine, assured, victorious,
slowly lowers us.

There is nothing before the Fall.
No sin is great enough.
There is no avenging arm to throw us down,
and no great hope to save us, except the ground
to gently break our fall.

V. Do I love you? Do you love me?
I cling to you as we walk away,
leaving footprints in the snow,
and the rebel in me follows the paths
of true temptation,
and reads between the lines;
sees all the patterns of our footprints as signs
that you love me, that I love you,
that we don't trace the icy path
to the pounding muffled beat that leads
the deserted gypsy now sat alone
and itching to see her own fate this night;
to strip off the cloth of her cloudy crystal,
her muddy handful, her comfort crumb, the euphemism
of so many pages, as she writes in blood, her minium,
her own star chart; a last confession
of how she offered so much and took,
but left no mark. And, at the last, she, dying, sees,
in the blinding light behind her eyes,
an office, desk, a pin-stripe suit,
and someone writing
in a book.

NOTE FROM THE UNDERGROUND

Underground.
Food, litter.
Nests fouled
and sour.

A pin-striped man
watches a rat.
The pin-tailed rat
stares back.

ORANGES

In my memory they are frozen.
One, in brogues, jumps high and throws
a battered foreign orange,
incredibly orange, across the native

jewel-green grass. Another student
is hoping not and hoping for
a mess of silly orange orange
to smear his face and hair and clothes.

In my hope, a cameraman's outstretched hand
enters the picture of a dying woman
in front of a desert.
He offers her an orange,

which she takes and painfully
does not eat. In despair
I remember that it must always, always
go to the child.

WEST

Out in the Styx
a swollen sun
plays on a drive-in
movie theme.
Unblinking, it watches
cars on the cliffs.
Crows swim
across its screen.
Watering like a broken
egg, the eyeball
hits the pan, and sizzles.

Electricity frets
its romantic glow.
Highly-strung suburban pearls
indicate shadow,
and sweat
behind the knee, and elbow.
The town phosphoresces
above a panting belly,
and open wounds
release their neon gases.
The empty hotel lobby hisses.

A stooped old woman
staggers at ground level
against a slick of slim-
legged girls on the razzle.
She is a broken neck,
a broken wing,
her coat's blades dragging
like feathers or knives.
There is a misguiding light
in the swamps past the hill:
glutted, shrivelled,
anonymous, vengeful.

DESERT CROSSING

(*for Tom Butterworth*)

At the lights
we do not move,
but I do not
switch the engine off.
You had wanted to
turn your face
from what you knew,
so we used the mirror
to watch the drive-in,
then pulled away:
San Antonio, poor Alamo.
We drove all night
through deserted movie sets,
many sad facades.
By dawn, we were
bisecting a dust bowl
with a plume of dust.

For us, it is now a question
of your words: yes or no.
Your tongue recoils.
I wait for the green light.
There is either an end
or not an end.

We wait at this crossing.
Listing doors
bang shut
then open to the desert.
A mailbox slaps
and the garage sign is rusty,
creaks and swings slowly.
Railroad points crawl
by themselves
from one track to another.
Approaching sounds
are turned anonymously
off.
I can no longer
switch the engine on.
Having got this far,
it could go either way.

It must be question now
of what is meaningful,
of red or green,
if by this
we understand an end
or not an end.

THE BORDER

The candlelight flickers.
Darkness is so much heavier,
and seems more desirable,
or pressing.

Goodness is lodged
between pillars,
and laughter is always
at war with the teeth.

Harbours are rivals.
They glare across water,
and resent the ships
they play host to.

The guard on the border
can't whistle, grows bitter.
He detains you,
gives an order, feels better.

We drive on into the darkness
huddled to the dashboard glow,
as the radio warns us
of warmer weather.

EASTER, WARSAW

Whores go down on their knees in the subway,
and beggars pray in the street
with children in their arms.

A bearded idiot unravels his wrist
with a rusty coat-hanger
and the smile of a conjurer.

He pulls ribbon after ribbon of blood
from his palms, festooning
the floor of the station.

A drunk grabs the hands
of women in carriages,
who whisper please don't

as he kisses their fingers.
Housewives, struggling under heavy burdens,
are crucified by pleasure

in their houses of pain,
while saints and martyrs
die of boredom in their charity homes.

Comfortable on their bed of flames,
only they can tell a whore
from a long-legged angel,

or pure joy
from the teeth and the smile
and green eyes of the Devil.

SIN

Death flies at me like a falcon.
Not as towards some helpless pigeon,
but, loving kind, returning
to my thick black hand.

DREAMING OF FREEDOM

We are cradled by night
like a fly in a big man's hand.
Half-crushed by dawn, we cripple along,
dragging a leg, a shattered wing,
turning and turning
in our frantic dream
of freedom.

THE FOREST

A pigeon booms in the darkening forest.
There is silence, and a creeping mist.
Things inevitably settle and wait
for the quiet crash, somewhere beyond the lawn.

A bough mysteriously breaks and falls
under a weight too great for it to bear,
leaving nothing, an absence,
a giving way to despair.

SPARROWHAWK AT DUSK

The stillness is the same.
Dawn makes no difference to dusk.

The day was a scorched hole,
a glorious breach at Antioch.
Shields, wounds, momentous hopes,
a burnished desert sky.

Or was a ticking clock
pacing kitchen, bedroom, bathroom, lounge.
Or was a hard-baked empty B road,
where the stems suffered the noon and slept.

Things have happened or have not.
Banality, in the name of God.
The stillness is the same.
The sun has grown cool again.

Trees stand in their black finery.
They finger the air, and clench.
Night blooms, roots feed it.

Virgin lanes are filled with priestly mist
that gently rasps the hedgerows
and smooth roads.
The far hills float like taken maids.

But my nervous un-nailed hunter,
still transfixed over darkening
desert battlefields and B roads,
eyeing tattered flags.

A fluttering cruciform,
offering neither death nor seduction.
When will you release me?

THE BOOK ON CORAL

(*for Tim Cadman*)

when me see the Night Train Yard
the Stopped Engines offend me.
despite all their Miles they are now dead.
leave me aching for Morning and Motion.
me need know how the Empty Carriages feel
to be just carriages.

me tucked up in Books
which only tell of Bits of me anyway.
Things are only interesting
because they say of other Things
which are just things anyway.
Books and Talk-Talk are hired Head-Hunters
welcome Robbers and Strippers
who Deceive us and Relieve us
so we don't have to watch
Ourselves undress.
they are just there to stop you and me
realising that We are just we
whatever Number of Different Corals
under the Sea.

but me happy when it come
when it come which tell me
how good and big it be to be
I.

AT THE END OF OUR LIVES

(for Ali)

We shall sit at dusk
in a summer orchard
beneath delicate trees,

the empty sky
rebounding
with our lives.

We shall wait
for the brown hand of sleep
to scoop us both away.

Something will be brought to us
on a tray:
a fluttering, an unfolding –

paper, birds, hands.
We shall read the lines
that lie in our palms.